# Own your brush

Practical tools to make your creative

journey a success

By Rebeca Flott

" I own the *brush*,
I own the canvas,
and the canvas is
unlimited "

Warren Buffet

## TABLE OF CONTENTS

*Own Your Brush*

INTRODUCTION

*A letter from me to you*

Friend, I see and know your struggles.

You wake up tired, you look at the clock and feel as if you are already late. Your imagination did not sleep. You have a crazy day, full of ideas, and too little time to accomplish them all. You may be working a job just to get by, but you want more! You feel happy for a time, but then you feel sad, you struggle with the back and forth of feeling alone, and being inspired, soon the day is over. So many ideas, but such little time, if only one day someone could see what is inside of you. You fall asleep with great ideas, and you wake up with even more, before you know it, years pass and you are so very tired of not being noticed. This book is for you, the dreamer, the artist, the Creator. I love what Warren Buffet shared in an interview, he said:

"I own the brush, I own the canvas, and the canvas is unlimited."

That was a drop the mic moment for me.

Do you dare to say the same about yourself?

All that I have to share with you in this book, I have learned in my years of being an artist, and I learned that despite struggling so much, I learned to own my brush.

Let's be real, can you relate to me? I'm an artist who finds that the idea of being a "starving artist" is not as fun as it sounds. Who says that we can't be successful? Well, we aren't going to acknowledge those voices. We qualify ourselves. If you are a chef, entrepreneur, or a mom, you are an artist. You may be the first of your kind, but no one will tell you that you are. You have the opportunity to decide for yourself what you are and what you will be.

So, enjoy the words from one artist to another. The words that I believe will change your life, as they have mine, if you embrace them. If you find yourself inspired while reading this, take a note in the margins before you move on.

**This is YOUR journey.**

How you see the world

You see infinite colors, limitless textures and you hear captivating sounds. Your vision is beyond the reality of so many around you, you capture stories in photography, and you revolutionize with ingredients.

You are an artist, and you create.

The voices inside of your head:

"Rebeca.....Artist can't pay their bills", "they starve", these are the words of my Dad. He repeated that so much until all his five kids believed it. Two of his children wanted to be artists; and they did anyway...but the struggle was real!

I remember liking color, paint, and theater, but in my head it had no value absolute, no money exchange. I craved to create so deeply that I remember buying the worst quality paint and painting anyway. The best way for me to paint was on jars and pottery in the backyard and mom would be upset about it.

As a young woman I had no one that said, "Rebeca you have permission to be artist to create." My battle was the voices in my head and my calling to create was a daily battle.

It wasn't until late in my twenties that I decided

to create. I decided to not starve but own my brush!

How did I do that?

You may be asking. I changed the voices in my head, and I went to work. I painted so many bad paintings. I practiced one flower until it looked ok. I cried and felt limited but I persisted, doing it again and again.

**Do not abandon your calling** because of your limitations. I'm taking the moment to ask you what the voices are saying to you.

Maybe it's things like:

Not good enough. Not originally enough. Not perfect enough.

I would invite you to silence these voices, choose to believe that the world is waiting for what you are about to create.

It's the brokenness and the lack of things that build us to do amazing things.

So if you're broke, rejected and abandoned you are about to change history through your story telling and through your art... through your courage to make art!

Let's say to yourself this message- You are incredibly gifted. All of your past and struggles  contribute to this amazing art. Your imperfections make your art empowerment  to those that came after you.

✍ "No one can label you, you might be a brand new thing"–Rebeca Flott

Have you ever thought about this? Every idea is a seed. Someone carries it, and they either choose to plant it in fertile soil, or they choose to reject it. Maybe, they reject it because it is not a full grown plant, or because they don't know how to water it. Maybe this book is like Miracle Grow for you, fertilizer for your dreams!

Every invention, book, recipe, movie, song, building, they all began in seed form, as an idea. The words you're reading right now, they are seeds that you can plant in your mind, or reject. The key is, you have the choice.

Now, you may be wondering how this applies to you. Well, in the most obvious sense, it applies to you as an artist, with your work. You can either create, or reject the ideas in your mind. But, let's look at it another way, consider this: you are a seed. Maybe you're a new kind of seed, one that has been planted to grow in a new way. You have ideas and thoughts that no one has ever had before, and that is fascinating, and worth considering.

That means that any label someone has placed on you, is most likely superficial.

Your job "title" doesn't exist! The truth is, you have the freedom to be whatever you decide you want to be. And, even more powerfully, you have the power and permission to change your mind.

So, what kind of seed are you? What kind of ideas do you carry?

A friend once told me not to let my dreams die. The first person who ever purchased my art, taught me something new. He asked me "what is the place that holds the most amazing creations?" My thought, the museum? Paris? Art Galleries? He said "The Graveyard"... The graveyard? "In the graveyard is the home of rich creations, art, books, songs, recipes and dreams that people took with them without sharing. That day, he asked me never to let my dreams and creations end there.

Don't let the seeds you carry die before they are planted. Let's plant everything we have inside of us and see how it grows. Pay attention to others and listen to their feedback, but don't build your life around it. Know who you are, and what you love and build on the solid foundation of those truths.

Permission to create, we live in a world where permission to do anything is requested. Can I set you free from this?

You have permission to try, to fail and to do amazing things.

I was working as an instructor teaching people how to paint on canvas step by step. I was so broke I couldn't do anything. I walked into Habitat for Humanity with hope of finding something to create. I also needed a gift for grandma, something unique. One day someone in my classes mentioned painting on screens I taught myself that is a terrible idea, but as I was walking through the store I saw a pile of screens and got one to try for $2 dollars. I thought this is my chance to practice.

My first intention was just practice, I painted and was bad... I painted again, still bad.

I Googled but didn't find anything that my heart was craving. I threw the brush on the floor and said to myself: "stop looking for someone to teach you, Rebeca you have permission to create."

I got some texture and applied it to the screen; my heart felt happy but it still looked bad.

I painted so many and they started to look a bit better. I opened an etsy shop and I decided to learn how to promote myself. I put in time everyday. I was still broke, the check out clerk from Habitat now knew me. Orders started to come in and I got momentum. I wanted to do better art. I did it, and did it again. I made room to succeed.

The opportunities were not knocking at my door. I persisted and persisted and one day I was able to tell my amazing husband "quit your job! Let's build an art business!" and he agreed. We were scared, we took the risk, and now four years later, I would not trade that decision for anything! The freedom that came with it, to create things, and to connect with people that accepted my art as a healing piece of their journey is amazing.

So why am I telling you this? Because you matter! Doing what your soul craves matters. Because something amazing will be born out of this season of hardship.

At the time of writing this we have sold over five thousand screens, all over the world, and we even teach people how to paint them.

To know that from our brokenness we can raise a banner saying "this is not my story where lack and sadness but building and creating."

You will suffer challenges, you will cry yourself to sleep, but there is a light inside of you that will shine brighter than the darkest of days! There is a desire to make a difference, to touch at least one person. I'm an artist that struggled so much that I decided to change things, not only for my story, but the stories of you my friends.

I don't know how to make things perfect, but I'll keep trying, because it matters to me.

"Art is the language that helps you say the things that cannot be said" - Jeff Goins

I know first hand, the temptation to limit yourself, to shrink back into mediocrity.
I started painting at the age of 12, but it wasn't until after I was 20 that I thought of myself as an artist. Growing up, canvas was unattainable,

it was expensive, and it was only associated with true artists. I painted on tile, glass, and paper, whatever I had available, and that's not the part that is sad, it is the mindset that I had, that I wasn't an artist. I'm here to tell you, Don't wait on anything or anyone to validate you. YOU got it. You don't need the right materials, you need the right mindset.

YOU have full permission
to be you

Remember this: How you see yourself is how others will see you. You must decide to see every opportunity as one to learn and to grow.

*Are you living in a house of fear?*

"We teach children to color inside the lines, and then expect adults to think outside the box" – Frank Sonnenberg

"Hardships often prepare ordinary people for an extraordinary destiny" —C.S. Lewis

I want to tell you a lesson I learned from a little story from my childhood. Growing up in Brazil, we were what you call middle class, enough to survive, but not much to thrive in the area of creativity. Mom had a book collection by

Monteiro Lobato, and these books were full of drawings, all in black and white. It was a very expensive collection for us, and many Brazilians had these books as they were very popular. Well, here's the thing, as a kid, I always wanted to color in them, but my mom said what most parents might occasionally say: "No, you won't color inside the lines, you will mess them up."

Eventually, these books were lost in a move, I tried to rescue them after many years, but never found them. However, I learned a valuable lesson from this experience. It's okay to not color inside the lines. Thomas Vasquez says: "No one ever discovered anything new by coloring inside the lines." Isn't that so true?

How many of us have those voices saying, "no no no, you will make a mess out of this." Here is your choice, believe and never color. Or choose to try knowing that you can mess up and eventually really enjoy the art you do.

I want to talk to you as artists about this, because we can be tempted to think we need to be perfect. If you think you have to be perfect in something before you can be an artist, and consider yourself professional, you are mistaken. I never color "right."

Today, in the society we live in, sometimes we have to be okay with coloring outside the lines. Of course, we need to have our integrity, and always do what's right and what is moral, but when it comes to art, I want to challenge you to go outside of the lines, and make something you feel like making, try, fail, try again and win!

> "To be an artist, you have to be brave."

"Whenever they think of what you do, you should be the first person who comes to mind."
– Evan Carmichael

You do not have to live in a house of fear. If you are there, open the door and say get out. Find a new place for yourself. Close that door and say: "I do not belong here, and I will not be coming back to visit." Right there, make a decision to not visit. When you feel your soul is craving fear, look through that neighborhood where that house is, and say: "Not on my watch, that place is not for me." Go be like an eagle. In the midst of your journey, you will find other eagles that you will be able to soar together with. Trust me, I get it, many times I felt alone, I felt unloved, sometimes people's words were harsh or painful, but I had to choose to move away from the toxic things.

Find people like you, the "eagles friends" and say: "Let's soar together, let's fly, what do you see? What do I see? Let's tackle our fears, Lets rise above and create things that matters because this is who we are "Eagles" in the misty of a world fun of birds.

# ✐ "How to not sabotage yourself

You don't have to be like everybody else.

"Everyone is a genius. But if you judge a fish by its ability to climb a tree, it will live its whole life believing that it is stupid" - Einstein

Let's talk about perfectionism, it's absolutely exhausting and unattainable to be perfect, yet somehow, we allow that to immobilize us. You may not feel perfect, and you may not fit in, but that doesn't mean you don't have value. With your imperfections, there is something perfect that the world needs from you.

I want to challenge you to think about the things you love that are not perfect. Pursue those!

People aren't looking for copies of successful people, they are looking for originals! Your greatest gift is that you are the only  you that there is.

"It's the gift inside of you."

Start celebrating your differences, your unique talents and your unique vision, and I guarantee you will race to the top!

"If you always color inside the lines, the picture never changes" – Anonymous

As artists, our lives can look quite a bit different than others around us. Maybe, on average, a person in a day may go to work, then go workout, then they watch some shows, but we know the creative process is different. If you are an entrepreneur on top of being an artist, then of course your life looks different too. If you are like me, and have a million projects, that is very different too. To tackle everything, including our daily lists, it can be exhausting.

I have noticed many people are addicted to perfectionism. It can be so alive in people, and so real, that it literally freezes them from taking action. Striving to be awesome, and striving for excellence is amazing, but there's a balance. Brene Brown, says it like this: "Perfectionism is the 20 ton shield we carry around, hoping that it will keep us from being hurt, when in truth, what it does is it keeps us from being seen."

# So, what's the difference between perfectionism and striving for excellence?

Perfectionism is when we believe that when we look perfect, think perfect, act perfect, we are going to avoid pain. It is so easy to live and act out of our past experiences. It is tempting to live in avoidance of any frustration, difficulty, or pain, but let's not choose that way. Let's aim for excellence.

Excellence shows up in our lives when we say, "I may not be the best, but I'm going to go for it anyway, and I'm going to do the best I know how, with what I have to work with". It's a lot easier to move forward, when we are actually moving forward. Don't fear moving backwards, you will learn, grow and adjust as you step out. You can change your life by thinking in a new way. Here's an example: You can look at your front yard and be frustrated to see dandelions growing, or you can choose to remember how you loved picking them with your Father as a child. That changes the view of the dandelion.

It's really in how we choose to see, is how you will experience life. How you see the world, is how you will experience life.

I want to challenge you, to have the courage to be imperfect. Here's a personal story I can give you about my own journey. My house, for example, is not always organized, I do keep it very clean. I work from my home, and my office is not like other artists who share their offices on social media. They have white clean walls, no paint anywhere. I work with a thousand brushes at once, and I have paint splatters. Whenever I think of sharing my workspace with people, I hesitate, because it's not perfect. I've learned to embrace myself, my unique process, and my workspace. There is always room to improve, but I'm not harsh toward myself for being different. I choose to be imperfect and show up anyway.

We can't let perfectionism stop us, learn how to silence that voice. Learn how to innovate, be creative. Have the courage to share who you are and what you have to offer. Say with confidence:

"This is the song I made." Have fun in just creating. If you're used to having a critical spirit around, you've got to learn how to block it out. This is very particular to artists. Have you ever had art in a show, and someone asks you, "how long did it take you to do this?" And, you struggle to answer? How can you put a definite answer? It took years for you to learn techniques, and to practice, it took time to master your skill, it took time to imagine the outcome of the piece. We know the answer wouldn't be, "Oh, it took me 20 minutes."

I remember when I started my podcast, I didn't even want to tell my friends I had a podcast. Because, I wasn't in the place that I wanted to be. I was tentative to move forward, and allow myself to be seen, imperfectly. I had to get over that. I'm inviting you to do the same.

Brene Brown says this, and it's so true "Where perfectionism exists, shame is always lurking." When we avoid moving forward in boldness, when we avoid opening the business, or starting the podcast, it's because there's an underlying fear of shame. We need to strangle that out, don't give it any air to breathe. Go forward! This is your time.

Give yourself permission to do your best, and show off what you created. Don't drop the mic, drop the brush, and say "it's not good enough." Give yourself grace, and do it again, and again, and again. I've seen artists give up on their dreams because they aren't "good enough", but I've also seen artists who didn't feel "good enough", pushed through and become successful. We get to choose our steps forward.

Have the courage to just show up, allow your art to be seen. Regardless of what anyone has ever said to you, YOU have to speak to yourself, "let it go, let it be." There are paintings you need to release, there are songs you need to sing, there are people you need to encourage, and you have the voice to do it! Everyone is so deeply different, there is space for everyone. There is space for you. Again, with Brene Brown's encouragement, "vulnerability is our greatest measure of courage." Courage is the birthplace for creativity and joy!

Many people look to be qualified as something specific. The want to have the label of artist, poet, songwriter, blogger, but, maybe you don't need a job title. Just because there's not a title, doesn't mean there's not an opportunity there.

"To appreciate the beauty of snowflakes, it is necessary to stand in the cold." –Aristotle

A lot of artists let their art die, because it isn't perfect and they don't feel ready. I heard a girl say "dreams, they don't have expiration dates", I don't agree at all. If you wait too long, they will expire. If I don't release this book for the next 10 years, the creative process will change. It will not be the timely message I want to share. When you have something in your heart like a book, or a business, work to release it. Set a date to release. If you don't release, the message will not be prevalent.

You will get better and better. It is like exercising your gift. The temptation for perfectionism doesn't allow you to do that. The perfectionist says you have to run a marathon without any training, so there's no time to exercise what's in you. No one is fully ready. This is part of living in the house of fear. Find the roots of why you want to be perfect, are you just comparing yourself? Become a creator, not a duplicator. I encourage you to own your own pattern.

Look at someone you admire, but stop and remember that you have your own voice. We, as artists never have the opportunity to grow if we are looking to just do what others are doing. Instead, boldly offer what is in you, even if it's not perfect. If you never feel it's perfect enough, that is truly something that will rob your career, your joy and your life. Don't try to be perfect. We all have weaknesses.

I had to go through exactly what I'm sharing with you. I grew up in a generation of artists where success looked like having your canvas hanging in a gallery. I tried to fit into that, painting on canvas. I looked to others to see how they succeeded, but I had to find my own way, my own brush. I challenge you to exercise your creativity, and your ideas of who you have to be and embrace your unique opportunity to create something new.

The Power of Collaboration

"We carry inside of us, the wonders we see outside of us" –Rumi

## Ask for help

Have you ever felt alone? Sure, we all have at times. But, there's something different about being an artist. As artists, we can be a little melancholic, that's just how it is. Many times, you will feel alone when you're creating something. It's only natural, because you are doing something new. We don't always have cheerleaders, and personal pep talks to get us through. But, we do have opportunities. There is always an opportunity for collaboration! There is a power in collaboration. When you are feeling discouraged and lonely, it is time to reach out to others.

Don't be afraid to ask friends for help. When you reach out, it's important that you be selective, don't just pick anyone, pick someone who is in line with your vision, passion, and direction. Go find a tribe of people that love what they do, and will inspire and motivate you. Social Media will connect you to people all over the world! I have made great friends, even though I have never met them. Sometimes, I even ask them for a phone or video chat, because I know they will understand me. Here's the thing: when you listen to their story, you will be inspired. You will find yourself thinking: "you are me, and I am you." You feel a connection, and a special belonging. We all need that.

I have a friend who is a photographer. Her name is Simone Severo. I love the story of Simone. She became a photographer because of experiences she had as a child. Her grandfather would share photos with her, and each photo had a note attached to it that told the person's story. In her child's mind, Simone would think "the people stick to the paper." She remembered them and saw how important they were.

When she was 5, she had a professional photographer come to her house to take family pictures. The pictures were printed and hung on the wall, above the couch. She remembers looking at those as a child and thinking, "I am important, because my picture is on the wall." Those feelings for her, made her want to be a photographer. She wanted to capture the best light in others. There is purpose behind her art, and she shares it with others.

When you need to move forward as an artist, you need professional help. I reached out to Simone. I asked her if she wanted to be part of my story. We have been working together for several years now. What connected us to collaboration is the quality of work , connection of the vision and the mission behind it. We both shared a mission to bring the gift inside of people into the world in different medias.

"There are people all around you who have the same mission in life, find them and collaborate with them!" -Rebeca Flott

Sometimes, when you walk into a room, you recognize and feel that you're weird, a little more colorful, you're bright, full of ideas, and maybe the friends you have cannot truly relate. It makes you realize how much you need people who understand you. Find the people that will connect to your heart and will understand how you think.

It's good to also make a point of connecting intentionally at meetings, events and conferences. I understand sometimes there are practical things that can tempt us to hold back. Maybe there isn't the money just sitting in your bank account, or maybe you feel it would be difficult to fit into your schedule. As a creator, you have to make your craft a priority.

I personally have a goal of going to 2 conferences every year. I have kept this up for 3 years now, and that is a lifelong goal for me.

Why do I choose that? What you get out of something, is directly related to what you put into it. I challenge you to pack your suitcase, and believe, so you can go. Conferences can be a huge breakthrough. In my experience, you meet wonderful people, but you also will realize the people there are just that, people. They may have reached some level of success, but we are all humans, all creators. You will have a faith rise inside of you, that you can do the same, if not even more!

Sometimes we label people before we know them, give people a chance to show who they are. Like Oprah Winfrey says, quoting her own mentor "When people show you who they are, believe them the first time" Maya Angelou.

Ask questions, and find out what they want to do. Seek to find out their strengths, take the time to affirm them, and if they align with you, move forward in collaboration. Don't allow the fear of hearing "no" keep you from asking! You may be pleasantly surprised with people.

Let them surprise you!

Here is the basic principle I want you to hear:

You cannot rely on doing everything yourself. When you bring brilliant minds together, you will not be held back.

If you know me, you know I like to think and talk about eagles. Eagles, they fly very high up in the sky as their friend. They are soaring with open sky, lots of air, and they are usually alone.

Of course, they could do what we tend to do: they could look at the other birds flocked together and think of how much fun they are having, but the Eagle gets to see things the other birds don't see.

You have eagle vision, and you're gonna be able to see things that other people won't be able to see. You have a big vision, and you can't share it with everyone, and not everyone will see you soaring above. Remember this: The vision that you have is a gift, not a curse. Don't allow yourself to get depressed because you're not singing the same song as the other birds, get encouraged that you are the eagle soaring above.

## ✐ Build a Bridge

"We build too many walls, and not enough bridges" –Isaac Newton

# ✎ Ask the right questions

Even if you feel that you don't have anything, you have something. You have the tool of your mouth, this connects you to unlimited resources. Every person you know, knows at least 100 people, and every one of those, knows 100 more. Be mindful of the relationships you have, and use the resources around you.

How many times do you hear people saying they are trying to build their business, and find more customers or clients? Well, it's possible they aren't seeing what's right in front of them. Don't be shy about your passion, tell others!

# ✏ How to add value

Hustle. You need to use your voice to make connections with others, but sometimes you need to talk less, hustle more. Don't talk about your dreams without putting any action. These go hand in hand. Cathy Heller, says: "We can't skip over the hustle." People who succeed aren't lucky, they work hard, and they work smart. Results don't lie. The truth is, you have to take responsibility for the results you're getting. Never ask for permission to pursue your dreams and visions, believe in the hope of them coming to pass.

Life of an artist is around solitude. I found

Cathy's podcast that has introduced me to new people, new stories, new relationships that made me feel like I could do anything. I had permission to make "bad work", so today I am willing to take chances. Cathy Heller had her own journey as musician, she grew in her dreams and exploded as an encouragement. Now she inspires millions of people through her podcast.

See yourself holding your dreams.

## Is creativity free? - It's not.

"You can't use up creativity. The more you use, the more you have" –Maya Angelou

Creativity is unlimited, but it comes at a cost. I was interviewing a friend for my podcast, she's a songwriter and a strong woman of faith. We were talking about how creatives can transition from dreaming to action. She said what can happen is guilt can come if you look back a year from now and think of your dream and how it's not accomplished. She said something that really resonated with me "...The answer to accomplishing your dreams really is simple, but it takes consistency." She stays consistent by setting aside a specific time each week. She said that every Monday morning for 3 hours, she spends time just writing. My practice looks a little different. For myself, Monday mornings 6 to 8:30, I am working on my podcast: interviewing, editing, recording and posting.

I am being consistent.I have set this time aside, so I am committed and intentional. Every single note on my calendar, I write what I'm going to do and when. I highly encourage you to do the same. Be consistent.

And also, once you find yourself doing the steps consistently, make sure you are putting your heart in it, be yourself.

## Be around people that can lift up your dream.

If you want to be a songwriter, someone you already know probably knows how to record a song, take the opportunity to learn from other people. I'm inviting you to see a balance between taking action, putting yourself out there, but also taking time to learn and grow behind the scenes. Be consistent in dreaming, you have to give yourself time to work on your dreams, but also give yourself time to just dream (like my friend). Sitting with a pen and paper, allowing ideas to flow.

Scheduling and planning your life is best. The care and consistency will create success. Don't neglect to Put time on your calendar for rest. You will find that your soul will be blessed.

Have people to be accountable to you, they will lift you up. Don't be shy about approaching someone you may think is "a star", the truth is they started somewhere too, and may find a way to encourage and help you where you are.

I like to connect with people through Social Media. I admire many artists and speakers there, and one time I decided to reach out to a best selling author Jeff Goins, I wrote to him, and he responded! When he offered to mention my story on his podcast, my husband was like, oh there's no way, there's no way he's doing this. But he did, it was tremendous for me. It taught me a lesson, it's okay to reach out to the people you admire. You'll be surprised, they are humans too.

For years, I would tell people about Jeff Goins' book "Real Artists Don't Starve"- a best selling book that impacted my life as an artist. He showed me that in order to make a living as an artist it is ok to do commission work. It is the work of others you will do that will pay for you to continue to create. For example, the Mona Lisa, was a commission work. I would say things like "as my friend Jeff Goins would say," of course he didn't even know I existed. But, he was someone I admired and resonated with. I truly saw him as a gift. He wrote what I believed in my heart.

Here's what I would suggest when you reach out: Start with telling them about how they helped and inspired you, don't start with just asking. Be a giver, not just a taker. Today Jeff Goins knows my story, and knows who I am. Again, all it took was some courage to reach out and be myself.

No matter who you think they might be, people are still people, we all crave the connection of a tribe.

Your job is to keep doing the good work even when no one is watching, find a system, continue to grow and give. If you are reading this book, and you don't give up, you can achieve what you want to.

My friend also mentioned and I believe it's true too, you've got to be consistent in giving your time away to others. If you only live for yourself, you miss life. Give yourself time to help others dream. Believe me you will find inspiring ideas through Giving, and Receiving. Keep the cycle going. This will create balance.

You will feel so alive by connecting people with their dreams, helping someone reach places they did not know they could. I believe it's important to reserve time to give away. We all have needs, and when you help someone else, you are inviting the same help to come to you. What we receive in life is directly proportional to what we give away.

Are you willing to pay the price?

Are you willing to get up early, put in the work, and overcome rejection?

Rejection is part of the life artist..dwell with but don't embrace it.

Are you willing to risk failure? I have applied for TED Talks, four times and they have not accepted me YET. But, I keep trying despite rejection, because I believe one day I will be on their stage sharing. You have to take a risk. I also suffered through many rejections wanting to have my art in shows, I heard "no" many times, BUT I didn't stop applying. Now, some of these shows even ask me to come, they want me to be there, because of the value I add. I didn't give up. How do I keep taking risks and not letting it get me down? I don't take it personally when I receive a no.

When you receive a "NO" say "Next"!

The power of consistency

I went out to lunch with a woman who has a very successful vintage show, she is brilliant. She said: "I remember you applying for my show years ago, I didn't understand at the time what you were." I got rejected over and over, but I didn't take it personally. When we finally got to be in the show, we were in the back room, where we could have felt "hidden" and like we had a disadvantage. But, we didn't, we were happy to be there, and we ended up selling so much of our art! Remember this: Even in the back, you can get noticed. It doesn't matter that we were rejected, what matters is that we were consistent. I challenge you to still apply, even after rejections.

Why would we live in fear, when we are called to rise up in courage? We have to be courageous. If you give up too fast, you are affecting your destiny. You don't know in 5 years what will happen. You have to run your race like there's no tomorrow. Work so hard, like you're gonna starve tomorrow. Have grit. I am cheering for you!

What is in your hand?
Time!

"I can buy anything I want, but I can't buy time"

–Warren Buffett

Remember how we talked about seeds? Every moment of your life is a seed. You are either planting seeds for your vision of what you want, or you are planting seeds of doubt that your dreams will not happen.

Every moment you don't invest in your future, you are doubting what could and will happen. Dream large and take action. Creativity reigns in what is available to you now. Don't wait for your dreams to come to you, use what you have and start planting for your future! You have 24 hours in a day.

I want to share with you a story, I hope it helps you remember how powerful seeds are.

When my son was in preschool he received a little bean seed from his teacher, she told him to put a little water on it and put it in the sun and see what happens. Well, my son left the little seed inside of a baggy underneath the car seat, and we forgot it there. Weeks passed and other kids started talking about how their seeds were growing, my son said "Where's my plant? ," here's the thing, you can't have a plant without planting a seed. Well, we looked in the car, and we found the little seed under the seat. We weren't sure what would happen when we planted it, but we gave it some water and sunshine. It started growing! We were able to rescue the seed.

I want you to remember this story because in our lives, we have seeds that need to grow. A seed is a vision of something that we want to plant: it may be a book, a song, a movie, a painting or a business.

Whatever it is, don't hide it! When you have those things hidden (like under the seat of the car) your seed will stay there. You have to take action for your seed to be able to grow, for you to be able to flourish. You have to expose your seed to the water, the sunlight, and you have to feed it and care for it.

# "YOU are the only one who can cause the seed to grow."

Friend, don't let your seed hide because you are afraid of somebody stealing that seed, or you're afraid of what others will think. When you plant the seed, and you allow the sunshine to hit it, and you water it with life and positivity, it will grow faster than you can ever believe.

One of the most notable qualities about people who succeed, is that they use their time wisely.

We all need time. We need time to give to others. I'm still learning more every day how to do that, and balance that with time to rest.

Also, taking time to learn, to grow, and to work. Time can pull you in so many directions, but I really believe that to be able to progress in any circumstances, in life, you're going to have to give and balance time with everything you need to. Yes, it's hard. The life of an entrepreneur is challenging, and not everyone will do it. But, you my friend can! You might be putting a lot of work in the beginning of the pursuit of your dreams, but it's important to remember, it's not forever.

Think of it like this: before you plant a seed, you will have to first prepare the ground, removing the rocks and dry soil. Once the soil is prepared you can plant the seed, but it won't grow until you water and tend to it. The dream is fragile, but you are not. By the time the seed starts growing, it becomes easier... you still have to watch it, but by the time the seed is an oak tree, it has strong roots.

You will get to a point where you sit under that tree and enjoy the shade of the tree. You may have to work a little extra at first to get the ground ready, ready for that business or that dream, but keep the vision of the oak tree in your mind, and one day you will be sitting and resting in the shade of your life. There is a time for harvest!

I really believe what John Maxwell says about time: "People who use time wisely spend it on activities that advance their overall purpose in life." Let everything you do, revolve around your purpose.

I'm still working on myself and how to manage my time. I truly believe it's important to have time to give, to give freely to someone, which means you encourage them with your words, you invest in their souls. You also need time to pray, and rest. I love watching movies that inspire me, that make me dream, so that, even though I am resting, my mind is being activated for something more. I believe most artists are like that, they need something to envision, something to believe in.

Balance your 24-hour day, by learning how to give to more than one cause and also have time to reflect, time for counting your blessings for what you already have. What I do today will affect my next 5 years, that's something I strongly believe, and that is the foundation I build my life on. Do today, planning for tomorrow. If you do a little every day, your future will be so bright. That's the key, don't let one day pass without putting the effort to grow the dreams you have. Now, if the dreams you have are so large, and you think there's nothing you can do because it's so big, that's absolutely a lie.

I was born and grew up in Brazil. When I was about 18, I remember thinking "I need to save money, so I can buy a suitcase, because one day I will travel to the United States". I was thinking so far ahead. Everything I bought in that time I was buying thinking "I'm going to travel, and I need to have this". I prepared for YEARS. By the time I was 23, I had everything I needed to come to the United States, I really believed that was going to be possible.

Small things you do every day can carry you into something incredible that is part of your future. Now, I'm talking about trips, but you can think about different things, maybe for you it's writing a book, doing little baby steps, maybe every day you are writing down a quote you want to use, you're listening to things that make your mind grow, you're reading other people's work. This activates and helps you to get closer toward your dream.

More than just believing in your dreams enough to pursue them, you also need the discipline to put action behind the scenes.

You must have the drive to infuse your life with action, don't wait for it to happen, make it happen. Make it with love, and hope, believing in your dream. You really need to honor your creativity, not passively waiting for grace to come from the sky upon you to make something happen. We all carry grace, and that is such a truth, but don't be one of those people that just wants to be found, you might be waiting for a long time.

The truth is, and I'm sure you've seen it in your own life, being successful is not just about having the talent. You also need to understand the business, have discipline, be accountable and responsible, pursue caring and serving others, create cheerleaders, and more. But, be encouraged, you can do it all, and do it with such excellence that you will be noticed!

Nelson Mandela says: "It always seems impossible until it's done. " There are things to be done, art that needs to be painted that has not yet been created. So, you can't rely on other people's abilities to show you how to do anything, we can model some success, but at the end of the day,

you don't want to be a copy, you are not a copy, you are a creator. You will establish a new way.

You decide what to do with your talent, you can't expect to hit the jackpot without putting your coin in the machine. A lot of people say they want to do something, to conquer, a lot of people say oh, I want... to be on TV, have a YouTube channel, write a book, etc.... but until you actually plant seeds you cannot expect to see fruit.

"Your talent is God's gift to you, what you do with that is your gift to God" –Leo Buscaglia.

I talk a lot about seeds, because I feel it's so natural and it applies to every single part of life. If you don't put a seed in the ground, you can't expect a forest. I challenge you to plant one seed and take care of it, then you can grow the forest you can see in your mind. Always do your best. What you plant now, you will harvest later.

Again, there's something to notice about successful people who are accomplishing quality. They manage their time well. They wake up early, they take care of themselves, they guard their heart. The people I listen to on podcasts, don't watch much TV. I like to watch TV a little bit at night, but I keep it very short, because there's so much to accomplish. If you live a life focused on what you want to accomplish, then you don't have to make a choice every night if you're going to watch TV, or pursue your dreams, you just live by the principles that you chose in advance. You have to believe in yourself. Listen to how Norman Vincent Peale says it "Believe in yourself! Have faith in your abilities! Without a humble but reasonable confidence in your own powers you cannot be successful or happy".

Believe that what you have to share is worth sharing.

At the same time, believe that you are also sharing a message behind what you do. You are a carrier of greatness, and it's up to you to have confidence in what you're doing. People will be attracted to your authenticity beyond just your work.

We don't always make decisions or purchases

on a product or service, but the who and why behind it. Behind everything you buy, there is a story, a memory, a purpose. When you create, it's important that you represent yourself authentically, with integrity, and also be willing to share with people your why. Beyond paying for your rent, food, and other bills, you have a dream for where you want to go, and that is your why! Find it, and remember it, and share it with people. Who you are matters, and the work you do matters.

✎ If you're not confident, PRACTICE MORE to conquer your fear or your block.

Without hard work, nothing grows but weeds. I do like weeds, not going to lie, some of them are beautiful, but they don't produce fruit. You want to grow and enjoy a harvest, don't you? You've got to put in the work, if you want something that produces tasty fruit, that has roots, that grows beautifully.

My encouragement to you is to be kind, and believe all things are always possible. Well done is better than well said. Show them, don't just speak, don't say one day I'm gonna do that, but go beyond saying, and show that you are living it. One of the greatest weakness lies in giving up. People who say they don't have time, are believing a lie. I understand what busy looks like, but we can't settle and give up on our dreams because we "don't have time."

The truth is you are letting something or

somebody else take the time away.

Give yourself a chance to grow, even when difficult things will happen. I have seen many hardships in every season of life, and while building my store was no exception. There have been times that It has been so hard.

One of my friends, who is also an entrepreneur, said to me, "How you respond to this time, is setting the tone for the rest of everything you do".

When you feel like you don't have time, you're setting the tone for your life, you are looking with eyes of lack, and not opportunity. What is your legacy on that?

Do the difficult things, while they're easy; do the great things while they're small.

"A journey of 1000 miles must begin with a single step" –Lao Tzu .

I used to do faux finish in homes, and I would start with the hardest walls. I would finish the end of the day with the walls that were easy and close. This allowed me to use my energy and time wisely. When you start with the difficult things you can get extra energy, and by the end you're celebrating.

"Don't watch the clock, do what it does, just keep going". That's a great quote from Sam Levenson. I don't waste time to watch the clock. I keep moving forward. Either you run the day, or the day runs you.

Now, hear my heart, some days are really hard

and you will struggle to keep going. The key is to not give up. Put the work and heart into your projects, and you will succeed. Don't think about your competition, there's tons of artists. There are tons of artists better than me, but I bless them to go and prosper, I think about the gifts that I can develop and learn. I try to not think about what other people are doing, I focus on my purpose, I have an urgency in time. It's important to realize you have an urgency.

"You are never too old to set a new goal, or dream a new dream" –Les Brown.

If you have a dream in your heart, you might think that this isn't your time, but don't delay any more. Time is a gift, you can use it however you want. But, if you really want to accomplish something marvelous in this life, you're gonna have to focus, give your time away, use your time wisely, like it's gold. When you give your time to someone, they better know it's worth gold.

The Power of Imagiation

One fear I've seen in creators, is that their creative ideas will be stolen from them. One lady I know, she makes incredible crafts, I met her at a local craft show and I said to her "I have not seen your creations anywhere, do you only sell at shows?" she replied, "Yes, I don't sell my creations online, because people will copy me" - so, she keeps herself and her talent hidden in order to try to prevent others from taking from her, but she's also hiding her potential.

Although people may copy you, I want to talk to

you about living above the fears, and the harsh realities that we face as creators.

We cannot live in fear, being afraid to put ourselves out there. We have to take risks. We can learn through the journey how to protect ourselves, but sometimes you don't know how to protect yourself, when that's true, all you have left is the power of imagination. When you see the threat, maybe someone is teaching people how to do exactly what you're doing, you feel betrayed.

Don't use your imagination to see people stealing from you. You have to know in yourself, you created it, and even if someone copied you, you have an advantage to make something even better. They will never be able to keep up with copying you, because you are ten steps ahead, using your imagination. Remember this, even if they steal from you, they lose a lot in translation, including the creativity, and the original brand. Of course, there are some necessary tools, like good, and detailed contracts or copyrights of your work. Sometimes, you won't be able to control that. What do you do? Do you cry out in frustration? I've been there, I've seen those same things happen to me. What can we do? This is the scheme of man, people who don't know how to create, they will copy. If you are going to be original, you can bet people will copy you.

Your destiny has nothing to do with people that steal from you.

I'm here to tell you, creators and artists that even if they copy you, you will have 1000 more ideas to bring forth, and with those ideas you will change the world. You can get mad, upset, or hurt, but you must rise above it.

I have learned to have mercy on them. Why? Because in the midst of this, on the battlefield, your imagination is the most precious and valuable thing that you have. You have to guard your mind, and imagine the future you want. If somebody tells you no, or fires you, or they tell you there's no way, your unique power of imagination will put you in a bigger and better place. Imagine yourself doing things you want with the integrity you want, at the place you want, with the people you want, that's the power of imagination. You will Imagine and manifest.

Hold your thoughts captive. Believe the best. This chapter is crucial for your life.

It hurts me to think about how sometimes people are so greedy, people are so mean, and I'm sorry. I'm sorry for those experiences in your past, or what you're dealing with right now. But, in the midst of this experience, I want to say, do not lose hope. Look up and keep creating! Your creations will rise up and stand up against evil days. One of the things people don't understand about creators, they are not duplicators. God Himself is a Creator, He is not a duplicator.

Imagination, I want you to take 3 minutes right now and just imagine. This is what I want you to imagine: You with the life you want. Imagine your house, clothes, friends, car, career. Allow yourself to dream.

So many dreams, so little time

This is for creatives. One of the common things that happens with artists right now, is that they have many dreams, many ideas, they want to do everything about everything, which is totally normal. But, what I truly believe, is you have to first, focus on something. Right? Something that is working. And, one of the things you should do is focus on your strengths.

I love talking to my husband in the car, and recently, we were talking exactly about that, artists who either focus on their strengths or don't. Most artists I have seen are trying to run 3, 4, 5 businesses, but it is hard to maintain and manage all of them in the beginning. We believe, you need to do one business successfully, building a strong foundation, and taking time to learn and grow, and that will give you an advantage: it gives you experiences and strengths to do other businesses, and to do them well. It is important to focus first, it's all about priorities.

Imagine your life is a circle, if the priority is your paycheck, it's how you pay your bills, your food. Imagine another circle around this, it's a little bit extra, maybe your Etsy shop, maybe it affords you enough to go on a weekend trip.

The other circle around it, is your long term business, where you are planting seeds. It's not gonna give you money right away.

This is what the whole thing about this book is about, as long as you are planting seeds, you will harvest. If you're trying to plant seeds for harvest for 10 years from now only, then you will run out of energy, and lack the supply you need for living now, and you will end up frustrated.

And what happens in this cycle, is artists tend to move on to another project, thinking that their idea is the problem, when really, it is the lack of focus.

Work from the inside out, if your needs have been met, and you have a little extra, then you start scheduling a little time working on your dreams. With the thought of many dreams, little time, you just need to schedule with the thought of priority.

I'm telling you, it's possible. Then, you don't abandon your long term dreams. Focus on your strengths, that means for me, for example, I like to paint and create, I'm not going to focus on theatre or writing songs, I'm focusing on my paintings.

When we talk about strength, that has to do with passion, but it also has to do with energy. I have shared a lot about energy in this book, the goal is to not stop halfway when you're building something. When you know you're working for something, the reality is that the results won't be alive so quick. When you know the dream isn't going to be, you can't stop the process, or the work. I heard TD Jakes share something, that I am paraphrasing here:

"Focus is so important. If you focus, you can multiply the things that you do."
- TD Jakes

I don't believe you have to live a life of just work, but you have to have time when you just focus.

Let's talk about the stars, if you just know the stars will come every night you don't look up in the sky, you won't notice them. They are expected. But, if you decide one day you want to focus on them, you will see them shine. It's very precious when you do. We have to intentionally focus on what is important.

My son is 6 years old, he was doing Summer Camp and they had a field trip to the pool and I said, I'm giving you this bag to put your wet clothes in here. When we come back, I noticed his clothes wrapped in plastic, he says, Mommy, You are very silly Mommy. You gave me a piece of plastic, He didn't know the trash bag opened, I just supposed that he should know that the trash bag opened. So many times, this is how sometimes, we say, you should just know better. It was a sense of humbleness, how many times in our lives, do you cover the clothes with the plastic, but then you just don't realize that the bag opens. Sometimes, when you focus on something you realize there are more opportunities than you thought.

We all need instructions from mentors you can find though books, Coaching is so important today, help you focus on your strengths not your weakness.

Draw Your Future

"Good intentions will never take you anywhere you want to go" –John C. Maxwell

If I could leave you with a summary of this book, I want to make it simple to remember. I've written 3 practical ways to own your brush, 3 ways to succeed as an artist. I hope they help you.

**1. Start with one brush** - Focus on one dream, one business, one endeavor.

**2. Use the colors you need first** - Start with what you know. Start with your why.

**3. Be willing to leave the work unfinished** - Learn to know when to let go. Learn when to pause. Learn to know when to revisit.

When you feel confident that you're owning your brush, you may find yourself asking: "I'm selling my craft, so now what?"

Work really hard to grow your vision. Ask yourself "What else can I share with the world?" Reality is that success is not just an event. I am constantly thinking about "what's next?" Life is in movement, we have to be moving forward.

Part of owning your brush is realizing YOU choose to you own your brush. YOU choose to remember that you are the owner. It is up to YOU to choose who you spend your time with, and how YOU will move forward to make your dreams come true.

"Everybody has Michael-Jordan-level-talent… at something. You just haven't found it yet or you have and you don't " - Evan Carmichael

Don't hide your seed from the light, be willing to be vulnerable and expose yourself to the light.

Stay true to who you are, and find balance between success and creative fun.

You have to balance true self and what people will pay money for. Some of your art is for you. Some of your art is to sell, belongs to others. Without selling, you can't make more. This is what I had to do. I had to find a way to express myself creatively, but also create art that spoke to others, so they would want to have it.

Believe first,

Share with those that believe

Share with the world

Let them see

Let them Celebrate your "overnight success."

Final thought

Friend,

As you end this book, you are starting into something. As I finish writing this book, I want you to know that the journey is more important than your goal. In your journey, you will be with the people you love, you will find your purpose, you will find the colors that make your heart happy. Above all, you must keep moving forward. Keep giving what is inside of you. Share. This is the legacy that you leave for your family. When you conquer one thing, remember to record it, so you can share your own story. I am here to share with you my story, I am reaching back to you, hoping to encourage you. When you reach a new goal, don't just look forward, look back at those coming behind you, and see how you can do the same.

You're a genius. You're the BEST in the world... at something. But chances are it's not what your parents want you to do. It's not what you went to school for. It's not what's "normally done" for "someone like you."

My goal is to encourage you artists, to own your brush and build a story with your craft. You have a voice, an art and something pretty special that only you have!Now go get it done!

"It's the gift inside of you.
Time to share it with the world."

- Rebeca Flott

*Acknowledgments -*

# "Because everything we want to create... we can never do it alone" - Rebeca Flott

Joshua Flott - "Thank you for believing in me"

Charissa Woodward - "You gave my voice words"

Raquel Ratcliffe - You have been my dear and beloved sister, and have been there for me my whole life, and I'm grateful.

Simone Severo - photographer - Your gift of lighting has changed my life!

Cameo Irons - Your constant support and cheerfulness brings joy to my heart.

To the Rossin Family - who believed in me and bought my first set of brushes.

Marcio Teixeira - my first customer in the U.S.A. who believed and paid for my art when I couldn't even afford brushes!

Edney Rocha - Introduced my new friend "ART"

To my son - You are my favorite artist!

**List of my very favorites books for creatives**

"Real Artist Don't starve", by Jeff Goins

"Purple Cow", by Seth Godin

"Steal Like An Artist", by Austin Kleon

"Talent Is Never Enough", by John C. Maxwell

"Your One Word" , by Evan Carmichael

"The Artist's Way", by Julia Cameron

"Don't Keep Your Day Job", by Cathy Heller

CPSIA information can be obtained
at www.ICGtesting.com
Printed in the USA
BVHW010606190520
579860BV00003B/24